This book is dedicated
To every person who was made to feel they had to apologize for their story.
You don't.

To those who stuck with me, season after season.

To those who fought for me and with me.

To those who tracked me down when I tried to disappear.

To those who didn't let me take the easy way out.

To those who helped me laugh in the midst of pain.

To those who cried for me when I didn't know how.

To those who kept loving me.

To those who stayed.

And most of all, to Jesus who did all that is listed above and infinitely more;
He who continues to redeem me.

Thank you.

"You're going to to feel like hell if you wake up someday and you never wrote the stuff that is tugging on the sleeves of your heart: your stories, memories, visions and songs- your truth, your version of things- in your
own voice."
-Anne Lamott

Preface:

Introductions:

I asked her
how this story
should start-
she replied,
"With an honest beginning."

<u>Nice to meet you:</u>

I'd like to think of this
As if you and I were old friends,
Or maybe friends long ago-
Just now reconnecting.
Possibly you'd be a new friend,
Whom I've decided to let
unfold the pages of my life
and have a look.
Maybe, we are curled up
On an old couch,
with hot mugs
on a rainy day.
And with a deep breath,
I crack open the spine of my story
The book heavy in my hands,
I glance up at you and say,
"So, this is how it all started."

Summer Days:

I'd be lying
if I said
it was all bad.
I remember
so many
sweet summer days,
staring into the branches
of our old magnolia tree-
Laid flat on the patio,
the sprinkler raining down on me,
watching rainbows filter
through the freezing water
and blazing sun.
July heat beating down,
soaking in the light
a little longer
to fight off the shadows.
Even though
I knew
my porcelain skin
would burn.

Aloe Magic:

I got sunburned.

But, the burn was always worth
The time in the light.
Nothing that aloe vera and time
couldn't fix.

Burns on the soul though
Aren't so easily
Soothed.

(Is there a form of aloe vera for soul burns?)

Silent

(definition: performed or borne without utterance // making no protest or outcry.)

Almost Normal

Mornings were slow and simple when they could be,
Taking time for a hot breakfast,
Saturday morning cartoons.

We played outside for hours,
Bouncing each other on the trampoline
High enough to reach the branches above.

The tree house our dad had built
Was a castle one day,
A pirate ship the next,
Another day a school,
Always room for possibilities.
Our attic became a second home,
Another adventure as we'd tip toe
Rafter to rafter,
Making sure some treasure hadn't been missed
In the dark corners.

Family dinners were a regular event,
Starting with a prayer of thanks,
Telling the worst and best part of our day.
Filled with laughter and warmth.

We were sent to bed each night,
With a hug from dad and a song from mom,
And sometimes a story if we begged-
A kiss goodnight,
And tucked in tight
And a bit of chastising for talking and giggling
Well after the lights were out.
And in our home, we slept peacefully.

Our home was a safe haven

Carved out in the center of town,
On a small lot in a brick house,
Which, in our eyes, held all the possibilities
That our imaginations could fathom.

We were loved.
Always.

We were happy.
Mostly.

We were normal.
Almost.

We were almost normal.
We were almost okay.
We were almost safe.
But denial runs deep,
And when trust is given
Instead of earned-
Usually, someone gets hurt.

And as we left our familiar city streets,
And traffic thinned,
And landscape changed,
Until thick forests crowded us in,
Until we turned right down that gravel road,
Until we were standing on the walkway,
Until we were waving goodbye
As our parents drove away
It all seemed so normal-
Until it wasn't.

Stay Outside

In that house in the countryside
There was a cabinet to the right of the stove
Filled with tiny jars
And lids to match.
I would sit on the floor
And carefully pick and choose
Which ones I needed for my explorations,
Because I had come up with one half of a solution-
To a problem I was too little to fix,
From sunup to sundown
I disappeared into the trees,
And made my home there for the day,
But no matter how I begged the sun to stay,
It always fell,
And with it the darkness,
That found its way inside me.
And at night,
I'd dream of home,
Where I was safe.

When shame set in:

I remember the day I was trying to climb
the tree in our backyard.

I put my foot in the wrong spot
and slid into the trunk,
Scraping myself from my knee
to my waist.

My dad picked me up
and carried me to the bathtub.
I asked to wash myself off,
He reluctantly agreed,
Despite how massive
and dirty the scrapes were.

He didn't know
how fragile my trust was.
He had no reason to wonder.
He looked at me and only saw
his fiercely independent daughter.
He handed me he washcloth
and left me to it.

My heart aches with gratitude and sorrow
when I think back,
to how I gingerly pressed the wet wash rag
to my scrapes and cuts,
winching in pain,
forcing myself
to clean those wounds alone.

My heart aches with grief.
I wish I'd felt safe enough
to let my dad clean me up.
It wasn't his fault.
It wasn't my fault.

It was the shame inside me
eating me alive.
It was the thought
that I could only
count on me.

I wish it wasn't real:

I look back,
And some things feel vivid-
While some feel like a dream.
Sometimes, my brain replays
And it feels like I'm watching a movie.
A horror movie.
On repeat.
And a voice inside me whispers,

Are you sure?
Are you sure?
Are you sure?

My left thumb
traces the scar on my left knee.
A little over an inch long.
Thicker on the top,
stretching into a thin line.

I trace it over and over.
I can't help but flinch
As the movie flashes a scene I can't stand.

I'm sure.
I wish I wasn't sure.
I'm sure.
I would give anything to be wrong.
I'm sure.

A Way Out

I watched our car
From inside the house
Back out of the driveway and
Watched my parents
Drive away.
And I always wondered
If maybe
This time
Would be different.
But he never changed
And I tried to make my mind
Drive away.

Think of anything else:

You pressed your finger to my lips
As you unbuckled your belt
Pushed me down on the bed
And then before me knelt.
I hear the quiet snap of your jeans
I watch your zipper go down,
Close my eyes.
Hold my breath.
And prepare to drown.

But wait.
We pause.
A voice outside the door,
Asking where I am.
My heart races,
Begs for her to run-
I'm too close to the edge,
Of coming undone.

"She's sleeping by herself tonight,
Time for you to go to bed."
If it's up to me I know-

I won't sleep again 'till I'm dead.

I begin the routine process
Of thinking of anything else,
Until the sound of its finish,
Catches my ear-
Button.
Zipper.
Belt.

Sisters, Secrets

We laid in bed at night
Held hands tight,
But your grip slackened
As you drifted into sleep
And I heard the door slip open
With a quiet creak.
And I knew
I'd lose
Another piece of me.
And I knew,
That in the morning,
Behind that shed,
While no one saw,
You'd lose another piece
Of you.
And one day,
I don't know when,
We realized-
Our worlds couldn't mingle
Like this anymore,
And we decided,
To sleep in separate rooms,
But selfishly-
I still missed you

Grandfather Clock:

Grandfather clock
Ticks-tocks.
One.
Two.
Three.
Four.
I hear you slip through my door.

Focus on counting.
Seven.
Eight.
I search for my scream,
Already too late.

Breathing labors.
Twelve.
Thirteen.
Trapped under covers.
Strangled in sheets.

Fifty-eight.
Fifty-nine.
Begin to lose...
Track of time.

Sixty.
One minute down.
A tear struggles free.
You
Rip
Into
Me.

Disappear:

In these woods I'm safe.
Alone in these trees,
I'm free.
And the forest beckons me
A little deeper every time.
And I wonder,
Could I disappear here?
Could I become someone else- something else?
Brave like a wild Indian?
Fly free like the birds?
Anything,
Anything,
Anything,
Besides who I am in that bed at night.

Heart Breaks

Close my eyes tight, hear him at
my bedside I hide under a quilt
sewn together with lies
The stench of perversion fills this place,
Here in this bed where my heart always breaks.

It slips out of my cut open chest
Which was sliced apart by his heavy breath
It slides through the sheets which wrestle and roar-

And falls.

With a heavy crash to the floor.

A million pieces- it shatters at once
He rips through my seams- I come undone.
A delicate soul, born whole, but now crushed
My world crumbles with lightning fast rush.

With so much breaking and tumbling down,
I'm shocked to hear that it makes

Not
A
Sound.

Only shallow, shuddering breaths are heard here
Only shivers, emptiness, and invisible tears.

Muscadine Haven

My sister and I used to hide
Beneath the muscadine
vines
And crawl through
That small vineyard's tunnels
And make a safe place.
With thick green leaves and vines
And as many grapes
As our stomachs could hold
But then the air always got cold
And the leaves fell
And our safe space
Our home away from home we'd made
Was erased
Until spring returned.

Tipping Point

I don't know how he knew
But somehow he knew
That I'd had all I could take.

So I stood in the doorway
I stood and I begged them,
Not to leave.
Not to leave.
Not to leave.
Not again.
Not again.

I stood and I cried
I stood and I asked them
Not to leave.
Not to leave.
Not again.

But all they saw
Was a pouting child,
Determined to have her way-
Which made them all the more inclined
Not to stay.

I watched them turn and leave
I watched them walk away
I waited for them to glance back,
I watched them turn left out of the driveway,
They blurred as tears slipped down my cheeks.
"Don't leave", I whispered
For only him to hear.

Not again.
Not again.
Not again.

I felt his hand clutch
The back of my shirt
And pull me inside.
I saw the door slam
Shut.
My back against the wall,
Sliding down to the floor.

Not again.
Not again.
Not again.

My hands covered my face
And I let out a loud sob,
The last I'd ever make
For years.
He grabbed my arm,
Jerked me up off the floor.

Not again.
Not again.
Not again.

"No!"
Little did I know
It was the last time
I'd speak that word

"Don't touch me!"
I wretched my arm away
Said for the first and only time.

Not again.
Not again.
Not again.

He took me by both arms
And drug me down
That long cold hallway

Not again.
Not again.
Not again.

I kicked and screamed
Cried and flailed.

Kicked and screamed.
Kicked and screamed.
Kicked and screamed.

That hallway felt
A mile long.

Not

again.

Not again.

Not
Again.

He knocked open that last door
One second I'm on the floor
The next
Across the room
Knee exploding with pain
Hitting the corner of the bed,
My back slammed against the wall.
Landing on the floor,
And I
Let out

One
Last
Scream.

Not again.
Not again.
Not again.

He scooped me up,
Tossed me on the bed.
And I'm willing to bet
You can guess,
What happened next.

Again and
Again and
Again and
The end.

Suffocating:

It will always be a miracle,
That you didn't kill me
Through not allowing my lungs
To fully expand
Over and over again.

But you killed me in other ways.

<u>Found: Cause of death.</u>

Ragged and rapid
You breathe over me,
One hand on my chest
So I can't break free,
The other hand taking
Grasping for whatever it could,
Rifling my pages
Like an open book.

Sliding your free hand down
From my neck,
To my toes,
And everything in between.
Soft, like a secret
Over my skin,
Or more like a silent scream.

But this weight on my chest
The flat of your calloused palm
Taking all the concentration I possess
That is until,
I feel your fingers
Jam inside-
And I know then and there
Something in me died.

You kiss me
Blow used breath into my lungs
And I can feel myself coming undone,
Breaths stolen from me
Never to be regained,
My chest screaming in pain.

Now both of our breathing
Ragged and rapid,

Yours from pleasure-
Mine from suffocating pressure.
Until you sigh with relief,
And collapse onto me.
I suck in full lungs of tainted air.

After seconds that feel like hours
You regain composure
And leave me a mess
Of indecent exposure.

And after you're gone
I scrub and scrub to get clean
But even with your hand gone
I still can't breathe.

<u>I didn't even know what to call it:</u>

Do you know
How many years
It took
To define
What you did to me?
And even when I found the words
I couldn't figure out,
How to say them out loud.

Alternate Universe:

I think
That maybe I thought,
"Not even God knows
This secret."

At home,
Most of the time,
Even I could forget it.
But-
That room,
In that house,
In the countryside,
Was a world unto itself.

Maybe, I thought
That the story of creation
I heard in Sunday school didn't include
That plot of land in the woods.
Surely, God couldn't have made
That house.

The stars and I stared at each other
Through the cracks in the blinds at night,
And as my soul and body ached-
After he'd gone back to
bed,
Maybe I thought,

"These stars are different
Than the ones I see
From my bedroom window at home,
This bed that isn't my bed
Is a different world,
Than the one I live in-
The world that God made,

*The world I'm in every day
That I'm not here-
God must not know about
This world."*

<u>In my bloodstream</u>

Days
Turned into
months
Turned into
years
And it all
mixed together
And blended
And then one
day,
I didn't know
where I started
And where you
ended.
Because
I couldn't get
Your pain
Out of my
veins.
But over the
course of time,
I'd try.

Chronic Disease

I had to keep living past you
I had to survive past what you did
Except that I didn't know how to find
All the warning signs my
brain
Decided to hide.
All stop lights frozen on green,
No boundaries to be seen-
So that even after you
Couldn't hurt me anymore,
I saw you
In so many
Other eyes.
I felt you
Through so many
Other hands.

You were just the first infection
That became a chronic disease in my soul.

Fracture the Quiet

When was it (exactly) that I (completely) lost my choice?
When it became too painful?
When it became too shameful?

I ask but I want to forget.

To put words on actions,
To confess another's sins,
Glass walls shut me in
On every side.

Each syllable of each word feels too heavy.

I slowly cut the stitches
Sewing my
mouth shut,
And will myself
To fracture the glass,
Say something
Say anything
Please.

Just one word could shatter the glass.

<u>Wait, wait, wait.</u>

Can't breathe
But I'm fine.
Chest tight.
But I'm okay.
Heart pounds.
And I tell myself,
I can wait another day
To finally let go.

In my mind
He still holds me down.
All that's locked inside,
Screaming to be released
But all I can feel
Is his hand on my chest,
Pushing me down,
Can't breathe.

I'm okay
I'm okay
I'm okay
I can wait.

<u>Where I drag each verb, noun, and adjective into the outloud:</u>

Why is it that I can't write what he did?
I'll use metaphors,
Skim around it,
Though I see it clearly in my head.

I can't say it either for that matter,
I try but the words are stuck in my throat,
Try to talk but only choke.

Maybe because if they're down on paper
Or spoken into the air
I can't pretend
That they aren't really there.

Because if it's written or spoken
Then it's real,
No more hope born from denial
No more chance
That it was my imagination with a twisted reel.

It was real.

I know what he did to me.
Even now I try to pen the words,
But I just can't.
I write slower,
As I get closer.

Take one step forward.
Just say one thing.

Come on, you can do this.

"Okay," I breathe out,
But not too loud,

"He took my oxygen
And replaced it with his breath."

It took years,
But, I finally
chose to
Speak.

Speak

*(definition: to express thoughts, opinions, and feelings vocally //
To give voice to.)*

Confessions:

I want this book to be nothing short
Of the honest truth,
as I know it.
And the truth is,
the words in the last
piece you read,
weren't the first words I spoke.

The truth is,
it took me a few more years to get to those words.

The truth is,
I never knew anything that happened to me was even abnormal.

Until 5th grade study hall.

Light Bulb Moment:

It was in the spring of 5th grade.
It was our last class of the day.
The school counselor and someone else that I didn't recognize rolled in a T.V. They told us they were going to talk to us about safety, and how to be careful, and situations where we might feel uncomfortable.

Everyone in class seemed to be equally mystified.

They played a video about a kid getting invited by a male neighbor to his house. Then the kid was sad. Then the kid told their mom that the man touched them and it made them sad.

I don't remember the rest of the movie.
The school counselor got up and told us if anyone was touching us, or ever did touch us in a private area or in a way that made us feel uncomfortable we should tell a safe adult we could trust- examples were given.

I never knew that what had happened to me, and now what was happening to me again, was wrong, much less a crime.

I was stunned.

When I told for the first time:

That afternoon, I tested the disclosure waters, I told my mom that my P.E. Coach was touching me.

It would be the only time that truly felt my parents fully believed me for years to come- I thought maybe because a P.E. Coach isn't too close to home.

She believed me
She took action
She did the right thing.

And that was the beginning
of my life unravelling.

What they said about him:

He's a good man.
He would never do such a thing.
He's a pillar in our community.
He just isn't that kind of person.
He shouldn't be lied about like that.
He taught my child for years, he was their favorite teacher.
He shouldn't have his reputation ruined this way.
He's a deacon at his church.
He's a good man.

He slides his hand up my inner thigh, leaves his hand close to the top.

He's a good man.

He touches my butt, leaves his hand there, I glance at him and he jerks his hand away.

He's a good man.

He drapes his arm around my shoulders and gropes my chest. Smiles at me. Pulls me in closer.

He's a good man.

My shirt comes untucked, he runs his finger along the bare skin on the small of my back as we sit alone on the bleachers. I want him to stop. But this doesn't hurt like it did when I was younger. It's really not that bad.

He's a good man.

What they said about me:

She's lying.
She's obviously troubled.
She has issues.
She could ruin his career.
She must have misunderstood.
She is ruining his
reputation.
She's lying.

I can't change clothes in rooms with windows.

She's lying.

I can't sleep by myself.

She's lying

I have to change schools.

She's lying.

I'm being bullied at my new school. This town is small, everyone knows.

She's lying.

I get called a slut and a whore at school all day.

She's lying.

My story is in the newspapers for everyone to read.

She's lying.

The lesson I learned from telling:

Don't.

<u>Spinning, spinning, fall.</u>

Remember those spinning top toys?
The ones shaped like a cone?
At first they'd spin so fast
They were just a blur
Then they'd wobble
As they lost momentum,
Sliding off course-
Then they'd tilt more
And a little more,
And a little more,
Until they fell.
And then they'd roll around,
Still trying,
Until eventually they
just
Stopped.
Then someone picked it back up
And started the spinning all over again.

I was that spinning top.

I moved so fast.
Pushed so hard.
Was such a force of life.
I could push all that pain away,
If I was just
Fast enough,
It couldn't touch me.

And then someone
Started touching me again.
And then I learned
Just how wrong it was.
And I spun a little slower.

And then my world,
Got turned upside down,
When I told the truth,
And I felt naked and exposed
For the whole world to see,
All sense of privacy stolen.
And I spun a little slower.

And then I got raped.
(Do you remember when I told you that my brain decided to hide all the warning signs for danger?)
And I spun a little slower,
Wobbled more.

And then one day,
It was all too much.
And I fell.

But it took a while
For me to get picked up,
And start spinning again.

And I didn't know then,
That as long as I let people
Spin me like a top,
I'd just keep falling.

<u>Let me tell you how I tried:</u>

I tried being good,
And I tried being bad,
And I tried standing out,
And I tried fitting in.

I tried to talk about what happened
With the coach

I tried to not care what everyone thought,
But I did.

I tried to do well in school,
But I was tired.

I tried to sleep,
But at night my brain wouldn't rest.

There were times
That I know,
No one thought I was trying,
But I was-
Sometimes I just wasn't trying
The way they wanted me to.

And before I knew it,
I was labeled,
One of the troubled kids.

And that label wasn't wrong,
I was very troubled.
And I refused to tell anyone why.

A Strange Game of Guess Who?

I was spending the night and it was late.
She was a long-time family friend.
I trusted her.
It had been a few years
Since I'd spoken up-
Maybe, if I was careful,
I could try this telling thing
One more time.

I edged around the subject,
More than once-
Testing.
Waiting.

And then she surprised me
(She was unpredictable by nature)
By asking me outright.
About that man,
In the house in the countryside.
She named names,
"Did he hurt you?"

I sat in shocked silence.
Stared her dead in the face.
How did she know?
Finally, my voice came out
In a whisper,
"Yes."

And I saw instant regret in her eyes,
And she apologized.
Said that she put words in my mouth.
It was like someone had thrown me a lifeline
Only to jerk it away.

"But.." I stammered, "But he did."
"No, I swore I'd never talk about it, he didn't."

But it was too late.
The cat was already let out of the bag.
And there was no going back.

A Conversation I didn't ask for:

I think my friend's guilt,
For speaking a secret
She'd swore for years not to tell,
Ate her alive.

And it didn't take long,
For her to find my mom,
And confess that she'd spoken
That name.

So, I was gently interrogated.
I confirmed that it was true.
He confirmed that I was lying.
But his memory was faulty now.

I tried to tell them what happened,
But it was something I'd spent years
Intentionally not thinking about,
And it was hard.

My story was fragmented and messy,
And I'd been taught that lying was how you
Survived these things.
And at first my parents tried.
And then slowly,
The support faded,
And the questions about what he did,
Turned into statements about fabricated memories,
And "We're not sure what happened
but something probably did."

And I kept trying,
And my trying
Kept falling through.
And I realized,

That he'd been right
If I ever told-
No one would believe me.

What pain does to us:

When I look back,
I feel so sad for my mom
And all that she had to endure
From all that I'd had to endure.
All we want is for our kids to be okay.
And I just… wasn't.

There was so much
That had happened to me,
I flew under the radar so well-
That when it all started
To shake loose
inside me,
I am willing to
bet
That every time she thought
That we'd made it past
The trauma and drama,
I would disclose something new-
And we'd be back in the thick
Of past abuse.

And when I think about it now,
She must have felt so distraught-
Because everything I told her,
Wasn't anything that had just happened.
Not like with the P.E. Coach,
So essentially, she probably felt
Very helpless.
Which essentially left me feeling,
Very helpless.

I think over the course of time
It became easier to deny,
That she and my dad could have

Missed so much,
And never even realized it.
"Maybe that
happened,"
Became easier to
say,
Than "I believe you, and
I'm sorry that happened."

I know I don't have to apologize,
But I am sorry they did that to us.

The truth was like a drug:

Once the truth was out
No matter how hard I tried
To keep it in,
The words seemed to seep
Through my pores.

I felt the weight of reputation
And I knew better
Than to be careless
With facts.

But so far,
It hadn't been me
Who had been doing
The telling.

It was confessions
From another's guilty conscience
And a lot of questions
That I wasn't ready to answer.

It still hadn't been my choice
To talk about what had hurt me
The most.

So, it's time to introduce you,
To one of my very best friends.
And even as I type those words,
It still hurts me,
That I shattered her world,
With just one sentence.

Our hill of secrets

The hill was washed with starlight,
As we drug our secrets to its peak
The delicate beauty of a quiet night
And the chill of Autumn nipped our cheeks.

Our universe shifted, and cracked,
With only God to see,
And she listened, as with a shaky voice
My truth unfolded and shook free.

The secrets I spoke
Seemed to spill out,
And saturate the ground,
With my words spoken
Into the open air,
Our worlds came crashing down.

Autumn breathed its last breath that night
Making room for winter's cold,
And we worked through pain
That was deeper and longer,
Than our years were old.

And this poem used to have
A different ending,
Back when I thought we'd survived
But it turns out, that as we grew older-
We could see, we just barely made it out alive.

Now I know,
we shouldn't have had
To handle that trauma
Alone.

In it together:

My best friend had to hear more
At such a young
And innocent age
Than anyone should ever have to.

And sometimes I wonder
Why she hung in there,
Why she kept swallowing
The pain I let out.
But I think maybe she knew
That if the tables were turned
I'd do the same for her.

We bore each other's burdens
As if they were our own.
If I cut, she cut.
If she refused to eat, I refused to eat.
Because if we had to hurt
We sure as hell
Weren't going to do it alone.

But we could also make each other
Laugh harder than anyone else.
We lived life together.
We knew each other
Just about as well
As we knew ourselves.
No subject was left
untouched.
It wasn't necessarily
healthy,
but it was all we knew to do.

Small Towns and Cigarette Burns:

For a long time
Just having a couple of
Close friends to talk to
And a couple of family members,
Was enough.

But the older I got,
The more tired I was
Of all the lies,
Of family holidays
That felt more like
Masquerades.
I stared at their faces,
And tried to steer clear
Of conversations,
Or comments
That hurt.

But in a small town,
Where blood really is
Thicker than water,
And the roots of reputation dig deeper
Than the sky of truth,
Every time another person
Told me how great he was,
It was like
Another cigarette burn
On my soul.
And every time
That I had to agree with them,
It was like
I was committing a crime.

Try to Find a Way Out:

Time marched on
And my scenery changed
Little by little,
And I found my own ways to escape.

I tried getting drunk,
But didn't like throwing up-
Or how it made the world spin.
I hated how it made me feel
Out of control, because I craved control.

I partied,
I found a lot of boys
Who thought that
Just because they were stronger,
Meant they could get their way
And that I didn't get a say
But they didn't know-
That I was skilled like Houdini at finding a way out.

The drugs I tried,
At that time,
Didn't help.
Nothing helped
Except solitude-
I craved silence.

And then one day
I was slicing an apple
And accidentally cut
My wrist in the process.
And it didn't hurt.
It felt good.

Where Cutting makes an entrance:

That endorphin rush
From that cut
Felt better
Than the numb
I'd been living with
For so long.

That cut,
Was like my first taste
Of welcomed,
Soothing,
Pain.

A pain I could choose.
My choice.
My pain.

And it was no longer invisible.
Trapped on the inside.
I could see my pain,
And his pain-
Remember?
The pain?
That I told you was trapped
In my veins?

It was like I was able to tell my secrets
Without using words.
And I loved it.

The Boy

And my second drug of choice
Was a boy.

A boy who wasn't scary.
A boy who said he loved me.
A boy who was shy.
A boy who listened.
A boy who needed
Me to be his escape,
As much as I needed
Him to be mine.

And boy, oh boy,
Did we sure make a mess of things.

But me and that boy,
We were young
And dumb,
And we really did try
To be good-
But in the end,
We were just trying
To survive.

Survive

(definition: to continue to exist// to continue to function// to manage to keep going// to remain alive in spite of- examples given.)

Fine lines and dancing

He was the first boy
Who taught me that lust
Could be fun.
That my body could crave
For touch
And it didn't have to be wrong.
And believe me,
I craved what he gave me.

I was the first girl,
Who taught him
That there was
A very
Fine
Line
Between controlling someone
And giving them pleasure,

And he liked to dance,
Back and forth,
Over that line
All of the time.

What we loved:

You see,
I loved
Gasping,
Screaming,
Clawing,
For pleasure
Instead of pain.

And you see,
He loved
Touching,
Exploring,
Pushing my boundaries,
To see how much ground he could gain.

And you know,
I think we might
Have both
Been in it
For the wrong reasons.

Never again, Just one more time:

But I don't want you to think
That it was all physical,
Because it wasn't.
We talked for hours
Fought for days.
He loved to take up my time,
And I loved having someone to give it to.

We loved to plan a future,
That we knew would never happen.
And we liked to fight about
Which sixties band was the best.

We were good kids-
His dad was the pastor
Of a tiny southern baptist church
Who preached salvation every Sunday
To a congregation of sleepy, senior citizens.

And we would say,
No more
Never again.
We have to have boundaries.

But all it took
Was one seductive look
From me,
And a raised
eyebrow
From him,
And we could make
A back sunday school room,
A great place to sin.

The End of Us:

The thing is,
I've never been one
For mind games,
Unless I'm the one
Holding the controller.

And I was getting tired,
Of always being under fire
And the pleasure he gave me
Didn't outweigh the anxiety
That I gained from his games.

And I was starting to like
The God in those stories,
And He was beginning to become
Real to me.

And that boy
Didn't like
That something else
In my life
Was becoming
More important
Than him.

And all of those things
Started adding and piling up,
And that is what became
The end for us.

One Perfect Summer:

I had one perfect summer
Before my fragile,
Carefully constructed world
Started to dismantle.

The kind you see in movies.
Four girls, who were best friends.
We basically lived with each other.
Laid in the pool all day,
And stayed up all night.

Drove around with the windows down
Blasting our favorite playlists,
Arguing over who's turn it was
To pick the songs.

We had inside jokes,
We defended each other,
We laughed until we cried,
And sometimes we just cried.

We shared the details of our boy dilemmas.
We shared secrets that we hadn't shared before.
We shared clothes, and makeup, and, well, everything.
We were the definition of being young.

We were reckless in the best ways.
Skinny dipping in the
moonlight,
And basking in the
sunshine,
And took road trips all
summer long.
And never got into the wrong kinds of trouble.

But reality came
back,
School started.
We took our last skinny dip,
Our last taste of summer,
On my seventeenth birthday.

And that's the last good thing
I remember happening,
Before I fell apart
And it all started unraveling again.

I Gave Up:

Religion didn't take away my sorrow
And even though I tried to stop,
I kept secretly going back
To my drugs of choice.
Always
Lust and Pain.

I was trying to follow all the rules
But I kept getting accused of deceit,
And I had plenty to hide-
But the crimes I was accused of,
Just weren't mine.

And my boundaries were
all blurred,
I didn't know what was
safe,
And what was actually manipulation.
I thought I was old enough to know
What abuse looked like
But I wasn't.

So when nothing I did
Was good enough,
And my confusion
Made everything unclear,
I decided that if they
Couldn't see how hard I was trying
To be good,
Then there was no use
In following the rules anymore-
And that's when my world
Split in two.

Sleepwalk:

I shout,
But nobody hears it.
I slip,
But nobody sees it.
A community of ignorance,
Swallowing my deceitful bliss,
My life is nothing but a lie.

I sleepwalk into Sunday,
I claim an empty pew-
My thoughts blur and wander
Someone says "amen" on cue.

I chit chat after service,
And it's amazing they can't see
That this is just a mask I wear
So that they can keep living comfortably.

What was your name again?

I kept getting my fix
From one boy after the next,
But for me it was more about control than sex.

Because by then
I was a pro at the
power play
They thought it was
real,
But to me it was just a game.

And I let them believe,
That I felt the same,
That they'd made it to
My hall of fame,
But honestly?
I was just trying to
Remember their name.

I needed a new drug:

I kept opening up
Almost healed cuts
To get one more endorphin rush.

When I remembered
What he did to me when I was little,
What I craved was rivers of red,
Flowing from a cut I'd made out of choice
Rather than the blood spilled from pain in that bed.

But like all addictions
The high was never high enough
The cuts were never deep enough
And I was making ones
That needed stitches.
I realized that I had to find
Some other high,
Unless I wanted to start
Having conversations about why
I was this way.

So, I stopped.
Mostly.

But that meant I went searching
For a new way to chase away the memories,
And that's when
Pain and lust,
Became one
Deadly
Drug.

<u>I was his drug of choice:</u>

He met me
Just when I was
Looking for that new fix.

The timing
was perfect.
The timing was
lethal.
Because I'd decided,
To commit suicide,
Through reckless decisions.

He had a drug,
That made me numb.
And I had a body,
That made him want.

Oh,
And did I mention?
He told me he liked them young.

I checked all his boxes.
And I pretended,
That I could handle
The darkness of that request
Just fine.

<u>I was his drug of choice whether I wanted to be or not:</u>

I took a deep breath and heaved open the door
I stepped out into the humid, mid-morning air
Glancing around the quiet middle class neighborhood.
I straightened and smoothed my skirt once more
And then walked to my car,
Exuding more confidence than I felt.

A phrase played in my head
Like a broken record,
It whispered frantically,
"It's okay, I'm fine, everything's okay, I'm fine"

I slid into my car
And with a shaky hand
Put my keys into the ignition-
Small half moons wrapped around my wrist
Where his nails had dug into my skin,
I paused and stared at them-
My skin was angry and red where he'd grabbed me.

My mind's eye flashed to the dark room,
Me, unclothed and rolling out of bed.
"I've got to go," I mutter,
Too tired today, too sad,
Wanting to stop before things
Got started.
He snatches my wrist
Just as my feet hit the floor.

"No!", I whispered in the empty car
I pushed the thought down
And turned the music louder.
The old speakers strained
Under the weight of the volume,
The song now distorted and oversaturated.

I rolled down my windows
To breathe in the late spring air
A little deeper.
And to let the wind
Fill up any remaining silence.

I pulled into a parking space at work
And bent into the back seat
To grab my worn apron-
My shoulder twitched with pain
And protested at the movement.

"You're not going anywhere right now
Come here and show me how sweet
You can be."
His voice holds an eerie calm
But I'd heard words like those
Enough times before
To recognize the sharp steel edge behind them.
I made a feeble attempt
To twist my wrist out of his hand
And his nails dug in,
As he did he jerked me back,
Grabbing my shoulder
With his free hand,
Slamming me down onto the bed
With such force that the breath
Left my lungs.
He pinned me down,
Though I didn't struggle,
I shut my eyes tight
And focused on regaining oxygen-
And then lost myself
In the sound of the rickety fan
Blowing in the corner of the room.

I shook the images out of my head,

And leaned against the steering wheel
For a moment,
Taking deep breaths,
Trying to regain the ones I'd lost.
Forcing the panic down,
That threatened to consume me.

I heard the slow tapping of rain
On my windshield and swung my door open,
Pulling my sore body out into the parking lot
I stood staring at
the sky-
Rain pouring
harder,
I fought for control,
As I silently prayed that somehow
The rain would wash away
The memory of him.

Denial is hurts less than truth:

Before I could see
What he did to me,
I blamed myself for my shame
I blamed myself for my pain
I couldn't see
How he manipulated me.
I thought,

I sold myself,
Nobody else-
I sold my body
I sold my soul
I.
I gave the keys to a stranger,
And said, "Make yourself at home."

I sold myself
Into grasping hands
I sold my dignity,
I sold my legs,
Breasts,
Hands,
Lips,
Everything.
One at a time.
I sold away what was mine.
I sold every curve of my body
And then I auctioned off what was left-
And gave freely all the rest.

And I begged to refuse,
Said it wasn't abuse
Just a choice that I made,
But,
Maybe now a charade?

To keep from facing the truth,
You took
What didn't belong to you-

Me.

<u>Back to the beginning:</u>

Though truth be told,
I was sold long ago-
In what was called a holy home
And I knew down deep,
That he still owned me.

<u>I'm fine.</u>

One day,
A friend asked me
If I was doing okay.

"I'm fine."
And I thought back
To the past,
And all the times,
That someone had hurt me,
And life just had to go on.
And I thought maybe
I always had been fine.
I'm okay,
Doing great,
Nothing more to say,
With a smile on my face.

I was okay.
As a little girl
When he crawled in bed with me.

I was fine.
When he made me
Say please and thank you,
for what he did.

I was great.
A confused child
Who didn't know any better
When he slid his hand up my thigh,
A look I knew so well-
Silent danger in his eyes.

All of this and more,
Running through my mind.

"No, really, I'm fine."

I'd said it a million times before
Feel the life drain out of my eyes-
What's once more?

<u>Let's take a moment to explain some things:</u>

I don't want this book to come off
As if I was some neglected child
Left to fend for herself.
Maybe in some areas I was,
But a lot of the time I left
By choice.

Things could have gone differently
No one forced me to make
The decisions I made
And believe me
I knew better.
I was taught better.

At that point,
I just didn't care.

I had become so good
At just pretending I was fine
And the fundamental need
To numb everything inside me,
Or to let out all the pain
Was stronger than the desire
To do what was right.

Back then I believed
That I was broken,
And couldn't be fixed.

People loved me,
Some people reached out,
But at the end of the day
I didn't want to be saved-
Just yet.

I made a new friend:

I had one credit left of highschool
And I was homeschooled by then,
So I was basically done.
All my friends were in school,
I was bored and lonely.
I'd met him at church
He was out of highschool
And decided we both
Needed someone to hang out with,
So one day I texted him,
"You need a friend,
And I need a friend,
So we should start hanging out."

And a few minutes later
He texted back,
"Sounds good, what do you want to do?"

Not the friends with benefits kind:

I don't even remember
What we did
The first time we hung out.
I probably talked him into doing
Something ridiculous,
Like going swimming in April
When it was fifty degrees.

The first time I remember
That I realized he was different,
Was when I was awake at 3am.
(Like always, because insomnia)
And I texted him,
"Are you awake?"
And he said,
"No."
And I replied,
"Do you want to go eat at Huddle House?"
And he texted back,
"I'll see you in fifteen minutes."
And we ate pancakes,
And laughed,
And then I went home,
And finally went to sleep.

We had a lot of Huddle House nights,
When I was sad and couldn't sleep,
And you know what?
He showed up for every last one of them.
He kept showing up for me,
And that's when I realized,
He really just wanted to be my friend.

A friend who protected:

He always seemed
So concerned about me,
He was so quiet-
I think since he
didn't
Spend time
talking
He could pick up
On the details
I accidentally dropped
Enough to put
Two and two together
And I think when
The puzzle pieces
Fell into place
He was worried,
As he should have been.

I also have a theory
That he would occasionally
Follow me around town
Just to make sure I didn't die
Doing something dangerous.

<u>A friend that didn't push:</u>

He fell in love with me
Much faster than
I fell in love with him,
I never wanted to get married-
I didn't want to be tied down.
But he never pushed me,
Not one single centimeter.
And that's what made him
Different than all the rest.

<u>A friend who respected me:</u>

Finally
He told someone
That he had feelings for me
And that night,
I cried and
I told him
That if he wanted
Long term commitments
I was the wrong person
To come to.

I told him
That I didn't want
To be in a relationship.
He kissed my forehead
And said, "I know."

I told him
I didn't date,
dating was all just a game to me
He kissed my right cheek
And said, "I know."

I told him
I never wanted
To get married,
He kissed left cheek
And said, "I know."

I told him
I didn't want him
To waste time waiting
On something that would never happen.
He kissed my nose
And said, "We'll see."

I told him
He was my best friend
And I didn't want to lose him
Over this.
He was an inch from
My lips and whispered
"I'll wait."

And that conversation left me breathless.

<u>He let us go back to being us:</u>

He and I went back to
Our normal,
I kept making
My bad decisions,
And he kept
Making sure I
Didn't die.
People joked
That we should
Get married,
He'd raise an eyebrow
And I'd laugh and say
"I'm never getting married"
And he never pushed.

<u>A kiss that made me think twice:</u>

One late
Summer night
I'm not sure
How it happened
Or why,
But I kissed him,
And he kissed me back.
And I told him
We were still just friends
And he said
He was okay with that.

I called my best friend that night
And told her it was the best kiss
I'd ever had in my life,
And that I wasn't sure if I could go
The rest of my life
Without kissing him
On a very regular basis.

<u>In case you were wondering:</u>

We kept just being friends
Without the kissing.
Well, you know, for the most part.

<u>My deal with God:</u>

That summer
I started really wondering
Whether or not
God was even real.
Or if He was who everyone
Told me He was-
A God
Who cared,
Who loved me,
Who wanted me,
In spite of myself,
Just seemed too good
To be true.

So I made God a deal-
I'd try to find Him,
I'd give it my very best shot
And if He was
Who everyone told me He was
Then I'd stay,
And if not
Then I'd go my own way.

And when I died,
(Which I figured wouldn't
Be much longer
At the rate I was going.)
If He turned out to be good
Like everyone said,
I'd be able to say
I did everything I could
To find Him,
And that He was a liar.

Narrow Escape:

I stopped caring
So much about
That drug that
Made me numb,
Mostly because
I didn't like my choices
Being taken from me
Like he'd done.
So, I texted my dealer,
And told him I wasn't
Smoking pot anymore,
He offered me a lot
Of other things instead
But I liked my control the best-
So, I told him
No thanks,
And I walked away
And now I see,
It was a narrow escape
Because generally
Someone doesn't want
To rape you just once.

<u>God came through on His end of the deal:</u>

God turned out to be real
And He turned out to be good,
And I could accept that He loved me,
Although I believed it was probably
Out of obligation.
We had a lot of work to do,
But it was a start.

<u>Love snuck up on me, I didn't mind:</u>

We invited my best guy friend
To the beach with us,
On our family vacation-
And I realized,
I didn't get tired of him
The way I had
All the others,
And when we got to my house
Late at night
From a 14 hour drive-
He headed home
And the next morning,
I realized I already missed him
And that's when it hit me,
I'd fallen in love
Without even realizing it.

<u>I decided I wanted him to stay:</u>

I told my parents
I could live
without him
But-
I'd rather live the rest of my life
With him.

So, I asked him,
When we were going to get engaged-
He said he didn't know
And stared at me.
I kissed him
And told him,
He should start
Thinking about that.
And he just smiled.

Love keeps trying:

We got married
Polar opposites
Really do attract,
We fought hard
Loved hard,
And worked hard,
To love each other well.
And sometimes-
A lot of times,
We failed.
But we sure kept trying.
I once heard a saying,
"Marriage is just two people
Who refuse to give up on each other."
And for us, that rang true.

Perfect fit:

We fit like puzzle pieces
In the night,
Your chest against my spine,
Summer night breeze
Comes through our windows
And silver moon glow,
Covers us both,
You mumble something ,
In a language all your own.
And kiss my ear.

Melt into you:

I push you
You pull me
You're quiet-
I'm out of control,
And we collide like fire and ice
Melting in the process.

Mapping Constellations:

Summer sun
Draws out constellations
On your skin.
I trace your stars,
And breathe you in.

I love how you love me:

There's something about
The way that you kiss,
The curve of my ribs,
Down to my hip-
That brings the corners
Of my mouth to a smile-
That makes me downright
Restless and wild.

Ours:

I have three families,
His
Mine
Ours.

His family is full of silence Like a museum of things unspoken,
Held with reverence, the untold.
His family is full of warm hello-goodbye hugs
That try to speak where words
Cannot be found.
His family is full of stories,
And laughter,
And love,
And anger that remains cold
And swept over.
Hurts that are quiet.
Apologies that are even quieter.
His family is full of silence.

My family is full of sound.
Like a minefield constantly exploding
Some explosions of belly aching laughter,
Other explosions of tears and pain
My family is full of snuggles and kisses,
And too much rehashing
Except for the things we don't speak about.
My family is full of ancient bombs,
That we dance around.
We speak,
And sing,
And not for a moment stop moving,
For fear that our circus
Might crash to the ground.
My family is full of sound.

Our family is broken and beautiful,
The products of silence and sound
Our family's runaway tongues are caught,
Then silenced,
And then an apology voiced.
Our family snuggles and kisses,
And is full of hello-goodbye hugs,
And sometimes just hugs for no reason in the kitchen.
Along with whispered
I love you,
I'll miss you,
I'll be back.
Our family is tattered and torn
With the battles and victories
Both present and past.
Our family is just beginning.
Our family, this combination,
Of mothers, fathers, sisters, and brothers,
Is broken,
But still beautiful.
I have one family.
Ours.

<u>Ignoring only works for so long:</u>

Falling in love,
And newly-wed life
Seemed to make
All those bad memories
Fade away.

But life settled,
And I coped
Probably better
Than most.

By saying I had moved on,
And that worked for a while.
For about a year and a half
To be exact.

And then,
The man who hurt me
When I was little
Died.
And a weight lifted off my shoulders,
Only to realize
That people can still do damage
Even after they're dead.

The damage that keeps on giving:

Everything my family had been
Holding in and
stuffing down,
All came gushing out-
Like someone had sliced open
Our jugular veins all at once.
Or maybe like the fragile china pieces
Which held all of the secrets
We'd been juggling,
Just all came crashing down.
Mostly because I,
One of the primary jugglers
Decided I didn't want to do it anymore.

And the fallout was more painful
Than it should have been,
And more traumatizing
Than any of us expected.

And all of those secrets
I'd been keeping inside
Refused to keep quiet
Any longer.

<u>Here's what happens when you refuse to deal:</u>

Those screaming secrets
Became a special kind of hell
That I had to learn to start living with
All day, every day,
Because they'd been quiet long enough
And they had a lot to say.

<u>I'd change it if I could:</u>

I'll spare you the details
Of what our family went through
During that time,
Because it's not only my story to tell-
But I will say this,
There was some screaming,
A lot of blaming,
A lot of pain,
And then silence-
And if I could go back,
Handle it all differently,
I would- in a heartbeat.
It's not that the pain was unnecessary
It's that there was more
Than there needed to be.

When PTSD makes an entrance:

It occurred to me,
That I was still in crisis-
Still in the midst of trauma,
When I'd talked to my best friend
About what happened to me
When I was little.
And that now,
I was being introduced
To PTSD.
Flashbacks.
Panic
Attacks.
Triggers.
Nightmares.
Intrusive memories.
All now flooding my world.
And I was doing my best,
But I was drowning.

<u>A long hard look in the mirror:</u>

Look you in the eye
Stare at the shape
The color I've always
Been complimented on.
Eyes the color of warm honey.

These eyes start to water
I see the pulse pounding
Under pale skin,
Color rising.

And I turn away from the mirror,
I don't want to hear what you have to say.

You and I, we're the only ones
Who know the truth.
The third, now six feet under
Is finally silenced.

I return to look at you again,
And stare at your mouth this
time.
These lips I recognize,
I see them smile on my mother's face
I've seen them pressed into a thin line,
I've seen them licked with desire and lust
I've heard them speak words that stick.
Now six feet under,
I've always had his lips.

I see those lips tremble
Begging to let the guard down
Pleading to speak
They beg to form
words,

But a hand-
my hand,
Clamps my mouth
shut,
And my voice resounds
Only in my head,
"Don't say it.
Don't let it
Be real.
Don't voice it
Don't choose it
To feel."

And I turn away from the mirror again
I don't want to hear
What I have to say.

That girl, she wants to be brave.
That girl, she wants to say
All that he did.
All that she's hid.

"He can't hurt you now."
I hear her whisper.
"He's six feet under ground,
You watched as they lowered him down,
You drove
back to see
The dirt
packed thick-
Just to make sure
It wasn't some sick trick.
No one's stitching your mouth shut,
It's time to speak up,
No holding back-
No controlling-
My god, just say something!"

I look in the mirror again.
She stares, I stare, we are one.
I turn from the mirror and run.

Who's really in control here?

Take a deep breath
Just smile-
No tears.
Step into two roles,
Puppet
And Puppeteer.

Both master and slave
These parts I play,
Pick up the controller
Attached to my strings,
And put on a grand display.

I am a manipulator of myself
I separate and detach
Sit up in the rafters with my heart-
My body down on the stage,
And with aching arms
Keep myself moving,
And make these strings behave.

Arms up.
Arms down.
Breathe in.
Breathe out.
Smile.
Side hug.
Chit chat.
Wave.

These strings long to tangle,
Am I master or slave?
These cords that make me move
Feel more like a noose
The cut off circulation,

And I feel the weight of deprivation.

Can I cut the strings?
Step off the stage?
And attend to this inner war I wage?

Take a deep breath.

Get it right this time

So emotional,
This isn't me…
Or is it who I'm becoming?
Someone who doesn't deny?
But I try,
Oh I try,
To bury it deep-
But no matter what I do,
It just keeps surfacing.

Cursed to remember
And so willing to forget,
If I could only
Erase these memories
The way that everyone
Asks of me.
So determined to
move on
At everyone's
request,
Feels like all they're asking
Is, "Are you finished yet?"

Surely it's possible
To just dismiss
To wipe it from my
mind
Though this crime
Was never mine to begin with,
But I swear,
I'll try to get it right this time.

<u>The day that someone finally asked the right way:</u>

"What did he do to you sweetie?"
Will she ever know?
Ever understand?
What it meant, to just be asked?
Not to be tiptoed around.
Not to be shoved to the ground,
As they turn to flee
And leave me be
To face this pain alone.

"What did he do to you sweetie?"
All that I've bled out on pages,
The cycles through grief's stages
The sleepless nights
And blinded fights
Not knowing where to turn.

"What did he do to you sweetie?"
A tear struggles free.
Where do I start?

<u>Learning to
talk:</u>

I'm good at giving
The bare boned facts,
The overview of these heinous acts.

But beyond that?
Down in the marrow?
The thought of digging it out
Pierces me, like a poison tipped arrow.

It's the details that eat at me
Like a cancer,
It's the words he spoke
That derail me, and leave me without answer.

It's those flashes of sickening memory,
That flood me late at night,
It's the knots it creates in my heart and stomach
That leave me without will to fight.

The picture of him biting his lip
That makes my skin crawl,
The words he whispered in my ear,
Make me shake- make me fall.

And I'm left alone with the details
That echo with no one to hear,
How is it possible? After all this time?
He's still my number one fear?

Flashback

I smelled you
And I knew you were coming for me.
About to drag me under,
To that place where I can't breathe.
I stumbled out, away from the crowd,
So that no one would see
What you still do to me.

And you drug me back in time
Making me deaf and forcing me
blind,
Until the world of safety is gone,
And I'm once again desire's pawn.
Filled with guilt, and grief, and shame,
And a pain that only knows one name-
You.

You.
Spreading my legs apart.

You.
Eyes gleaming, smile sliding on your face in the dark.

You.
Lowering your head.

You.
With your forehead on my stomach,
As I claw the sheets on this bed.

And I fight back a scream.
And you're killing me.

You.
Biting where no one would think to look.

You.
Telling me I'd better be still as I trembled and shook.

You.
Trace your finger from my neck to below, like you're slicing me open.

You.
Shattering me until there's nothing left to be broken.

And this waking nightmare,
So much more vivid than
Any dream I've had.

Choking on your poison.
Until I heave, convulse,
Rip this dream at its seams.

Shaking as I pick up this shovel
To dig furiously as my panic doubles
Slam the casket shut with a bang
And bury you back where you belong
Six feet under ground in your grave.

And I take a deep breath and count
Just like I always have
Until you trickle back out of me
Down through the floor
Dripping through cracks.

One.
Two.
Three.
Hold my breath.
Four.
I hear you slip back out my door
And leave me to resew the seams

You've torn.
And wonder how it is that even from the grave,
You still get to have your way.

<u>A well-oiled wheel:</u>

Through all the ways I learned to be quiet
I didn't get to pick and choose
What needs I was quiet about
So, it turned into all of them.

I listened to people talk about others,
I don't know how many times
I've heard, "They are so strong, a survivor."
Because they know,
That person's story has been told.
And when the screw up
No one told them to just toughen up,
Because they knew
They were probably just working through
A wound.

So, I learned to go through life
Noticed but unnoticed.
Trying to always be a help,
And never an inconvenience.
If I never voiced a need,
Then I'd never be rejected,
I'd never have a reason
For someone to resent me.

I didn't like the idea of being a squeaky wheel,
But sometimes I long to be.

A Letter to my husband:

Hey babe,
I know you're confused
I know you don't get it.
I know that my nightmares,
My flash backs,
My panic attacks,
Come suddenly, violently, and without warning.
But we both know they don't come
Without cause.
I know that you know that I'm hurt,
And just like always,
You've just kept staying steady,
Kept loving,
Kept showing up for me,
You know that this girl-
However messy,
However fractured and torn-
Is yours.
I know I might not look my best right now,
But I know that you know,
I'm still yours.
And we're going to make it through this.

<u>What I wanted to say to my mom at the time:</u>

Why wouldn't you just listen?
I pitched a fit, and screamed, and cried,
You would have thought somebody died.
Someone did, you just couldn't see-
The person who died,
Was me.

I died, over and over again-
And you just wouldn't open your eyes,
Drove away from that house in the countryside
While I figured out how to survive.

And I know you're tired of this same old verse,
Where every other line rhymes,
It must feel like a curse-
To have such a hideous monster,
Never fade away.
Must be hard for you, to keep it stuffed in the closet,
To see the scars marked into your child every single damn day.
I bet it's so tiring to keep it all in the dark,
Because I know it must hurt you
If it hurts my heart.

You listen to everyone else.
Just give me a chance,
To tell you how I've felt,
Through tears
Through years
Through sorrow
Through pain,
Please just listen,
I promise to keep it short, but not sweet
And for you, I won't name names.
But I need you,
To hear me.

What life looked like a year after I wrote that last poem:

I have two babies
Kicking around in my belly.
My feet are propped up
On my mom's lap,
As she tells me
About how dark
That time was for her.
How she almost gave up,
Because life wouldn't be worth living
If there was no us.

And my heart broke,
I told her how sorry I was
That the fallout had been so brutal,
And if I could go back and change it
I would.

And we forgave each other.
I was finding that it was easier
To forgive someone when you know
That they love you,
And when you know,
That they're sorry.

And I could finally see,
That she had been young back then too,
And too trusting,
And yes, it was a mistake
And no, it's not one she could unmake.
But she was sorry.
And we were talking.
And we were
trying.

And we were
loving each other
through
the wreckage,
And even though it may have taken years,
We were finally feeling,
Like there was a light
At the end of the long dark tunnel

The power of secrecy:

I've tried to fly so many times
Shackled to the ground
Chains rattle as I pace.
How I've learned to live
Is a damn disgrace.

I get a running start to soar
And leap so high from the earth,
Too quickly reminded of how I'm tethered.
And how this soul has become so weathered.

These shackles that have no key,
Attached to my wrists,
To my neck,
And my feet,
Spider away from my body,
One lock linked to another chain
And each branded with a name.

Abuse, Self-injury, Nightmares, Rape.
Against my wrists the metal scrapes.
Slut, Worthless, Disappointment, Regret.
Four more names that I'll never forget.
Into my ankles the bonds dig deep.
The lock around my neck,
Bears one burden under which the others fall
The suffocating, all consuming, heavy weight
Of shame.
The sin of what he did,
Now my job to hide
To bottle it up with a strong tight lid,
Which no one will ever find.

Covering these shackles and chains
With beautiful scarves and gloves,

And a little makeup for my face,
Learn to sit pretty,
Draw no attention to the chains
That hold me still,
And meet weekly with my
Self-blame committee.

But, in the night, when no one can see
I'll gather my shackles and sit at His feet.
He sees the pain and it doesn't scare Him
A man well acquainted with grief and sin-
I strip off the garments that cover my chains
And pour out my heart
And pour out my pain,
And He waits.
So patiently.
Never willing to force me,
For the night that the words fall from my lips,
"Set me free."
But day breaks, and I wait a day longer.

Trying to find the truth:

I've been told that this body is a temple
A vessel which I thought
The only purpose was to degrade,
To shred to pieces the life inside
And bury in a shallow grave.
Through thievery and force,
I was brought to be
Constantly at self-war.

Every day a battle,
To find the truth about this body
And what of its
purpose
And what of its
destiny,
May have been robbed by thieves.
For by them I thought
Was this clay vessel consistently shattered,
And to be repaired so often,
Was too high a cost.

Too broken, too scared.
I built the highest wall I could,
Put this temple on lock down,
Poured grief into the moat I'd dug.
And found sorrow to only abound.

I barred the door,
And tried to lose myself
In hallways filled with vast unknowns
And locked the doors on phantom moans.

For my sin, I attempted to atone.
Little did I know,
That God doesn't leave,

Even a wandering heart, alone.

In deepest night I cried,
Lost in myself and chained to the night.
"God you're the only one
Who can set me free,
The only one who can break these chains
That are holding me."

You burst down the door
I had barred
And shined holy light
Into all of my dark
Yet, so tender and gentle,
You consecrated again this temple.

I took a sabbatical.

I took a four year long break
From my past.
Not forgetting,
Not holding memories hostage
Just being,
Just mending
And strengthening
My relationships.
My mom.
My dad.
My sisters.
All needed mending.

To be honest,
I thought I was done.
I thought I'd put it all
behind me.
I had three sweet
babies
That I was very busy with.
But every once in a while,
Something would happen
That would knock the wind out of me-
It could be big or small,
But that trigger would pull and fire a shot
And I was instantly reminded
Of all I had never forgot.

Pressure started building in me,
Anxiety that was absolutely unrelenting.
The memories that I never forgot
Came closer and quicker to mind
And no matter how hard I tried,
It got harder every time.

I started trying to talk about
The details of what happened,
And realized it was all I could do,
To even say what really happened out loud.
I wanted to be cold- because the pain was hot.
I wanted to be clinical- easier that way.
I wanted to be accurate- never to be labeled a liar.
But the words still stuck in my throat.

Am I crazy?

There were all these things
I'd never said out loud,
And I started wondering-
If they were real,
Or if I was crazy.

But as I talked to others,
We realized
Our fabricated
memories
Couldn't be so similar
And not be real.
But you have no idea,
Just how bad,
I wanted it not to be real.

I tried to talk my way out
Of reality,
A thousand different ways,
But there was just no changing it
It was there to stay.

Past, Present, Future

I looked at my children and husband
And I knew,
I had to be healthy
If not for me then for them.

But I also had to do it for me,
To show my kids
That we can do hard things,
And make it out
The other side.

I decided
It was time,
To finally learn
To breathe.

Breathe

*(definition: To take air in,
and expel it from the lungs// to inhale
and exhale freely// to feel free from restraint.)*

Shouldn't this come naturally?

No one teaches
Someone to
breathe
Your lungs
inhaling
And exhaling is just
Natural.

But the way
He made
Me struggle to breathe
With his hand
On my chest
Holding me
down Forcing
my lungs
To not fully
Expand

Made it nearly
Impossible
To take a deep
Breath
For the rest of my
Life.

How do I learn to breathe?

Terminally Unique:

Sometimes
A lot of times
Through practice
And self-discipline
From an early age
I got very good
At holding myself together
At not totally falling apart
Arms wrapped around myself
As tight as I could
I lived in a world
Where I believed
I required less oxygen
Than everyone else.

<u>Indulge in oxygen:</u>

When all the things
I didn't want to feel
Or remember
Started climbing
To the surface
Demanding to be heard and seen
I'd indulge myself
With a deeper breath,
Than usual.
So that everything inside
Would settle down
Until the next time.

<u>The honest fear:</u>

Maybe I was afraid
To breathe deep
Because if I inhaled
Too much oxygen
I'd exhale a scream.

One of many metaphors my therapist used:

My therapist said
That I was like someone
Who had been hiding
Behind a curtain
Their whole life.
And sometimes,
I'd try to peek around it
And most times
I'd gotten shut down
When I did.

So now,
I was having to learn
To live with my curtains
Opened just a little-
And with time
I could maybe
Learn to live
Standing in front
Of the curtain.

I like my curtains
Closed tight,
Thank you very much.

<u>But wasn't I fine?</u>

Just months ago I'd been
Fine.

Not in the memory-soaked madness of
Now.

Everything suddenly shifted so
Fast.

I tried to put on a brave face but my insides were
Crumbling.

All the things I'd chosen not to think about were
Back.

But you know what fine means? It means you're
Not.

And I could talk about anything except what happened

In that house

In the countryside.

Everything tied back

To that.

Talking about it feels like stripping naked:

Picture this-
You're standing in front of someone
So panicked you're about to run,
But you decide
That it's long past time,
To let the things that haunt you
See some light.
So someone watches,
While you strip each piece of clothing off
One
By
One.
Flinching as you shrug out of another sleeve,
Whimpering as you kick off your jeans-
Every undergarment, bottom to top
Has to come off.
You try to cover up
But what's done is done
They can't un-see
Your naked body.
And oh God, you hope they'll understand,
And you pray that they'll be a safe place to land.
The hardest part
Is that they
Get to stay
Dressed.
But you count your lucky stars,
Every time you realize
all that they're looking at
Is your heart.

Another way to look at it:

You know what talking about
The details
Is also like?

It's like taking a hammer
In your right hand,
And deciding
You're going to
Smash your left hand
On purpose.

And you keep
Prepping yourself,
Going over it in your mind,
And you bring your hand up
Ready to swing down-
And then you chicken out.

And you repeat
That process of the
Almost swing,
Until finally you just close your eyes
And sort of hope
That you'll somehow
Miss the target,

And you wonder, will the talking
Ever get easier?

Taught Silence:

I've realized
That my brain
Was wired
To silence pain.

I've thought
About how my mind
Was taught
To hold shame tight.

But I've seen
That when I talk
I'm allowing mending
To another broken spot.

A revelation I needed:

I still had trouble sometimes
Believing that what I remembered
Was real,
And one day I realized-
If I'd made it all up,
Some part of me would know,
And wouldn't that knowing part,
Somehow make it easier to
Say it out loud?
Wouldn't it be easier to voice
If it was never true to begin with?
The truth is what hurts the worst.
And if that's not enough
To convince me,
I can always trace
The scar on me knee,
From that first time
That he unraveled me.

I'm sure.
I wish I wasn't sure.
I'm sure.
I would give anything to be wrong.
I'm sure.

Process Poetry:

I've used the metaphor "unraveled" a lot of times.
Like I was undone, unspun...
Why is that?
Maybe I think of myself as starting out life
With strong stiches- all fresh and new,
Straight out of the sewing machine,
And what he did, started as picking at a seam-
Tugging it loose...
Another night, tug here,
Another touch, tug there,
And then over time my stitching
Was being held together by the sheer will power
Of five-year-old me.
And when he did what he did that day,
he grabbed a thread and jerked it out
With such a force
That I didn't stand a chance.

Something in me fell apart,
So entirely.
So completely.
And that's what I mean
When I say he unraveled me.

But from there on out,
He just started cutting seams.
No reason to waste time
With pulling at them.

What he did:

That day,
That day that I keep
Going back to.
The day I kicked and screamed.
The day my knee split open
The day my voice was stolen
That day and every time after.
It took me so long to say,
What he did that day,
I didn't want to see it-
Didn't want
to call it
What it was.
My brain
Begged me not
To look at it.
My mind
Pleaded with me
Not to think
About that day-
Because it new,
That if I ever spoke it
Out loud-
Someone would say
It was
Rape.

Speak it once, twice, how many times?

Every thread that he cut,
He re-used to sew
My mouth shut.

But every word
That I spoke
Seemed to serve,
As a seam cutter-

And I'd said it
Once
I'd said it
Twice
And I don't think
You heard me stutter.

-That is, once I could get the words out.

<u>Turns out talking does do some good:</u>

I'd been so determined
Not to define what happened
Using that word.

But then the more
That I spoke it,
Or wrote it-
I realized,

I was breathing
Just a little more
Deep than before.

A second letter to my husband:

Hey love,
I know you thought
We were done with this-
Believe me so did I.
Thank you for never
Making me feel guilty
For a story I never chose,
Thank you for never
Asking me to apologize
For not "getting over it"
As fast as I want to.
Because every time I question you,
Every time I ask, if you wish I wasn't me
You stroke my cheek, and say
"I'd pick you, no matter what, every day."
And we both have our problems
From our fractured families,
But we are crazy about each other-
After all these years,
You are still the safest place I know.
Intertwined in your arms at night
My lips brush yours and I whisper,
"Sometimes you are the best medicine
For me."
Always, always,
You are for me-
And I love you more
Than I ever thought possible.

Maybe, Maybe, Maybe:

Maybe it's okay to need,
Part of love's mystery
To show you who I really am
To reach and grab
Your outstretched hand-
Where talk and honesty meet.
And this love
Becomes
A two-way street.

Slowly, slowly, but surely:

The world grows quiet around me
Peace within the storm
Physician's hands are mending me
In the places I've been torn.
No morphine to keep out the pain,
This healing comes
By a different name.
Needle and thread in Your hand,
Uncover my soul and see beauty in wreckage
The way that only You can.
You wipe the tears that slide down my cheeks
As I hand over these secrets I've been forced to keep.
And show You the dark, and ugly sin
I've hidden so well, buried deep within.

You assess every gaping wound,
Take note of every broken place,
And then reset the bones
And stitch closed the cuts,
Threads woven together of mercy and grace.

Slowly, the heaviness is lifting,
This way of life I've always known
Finally is shifting.

Ragdoll:

I told you how when I was small
I had fresh seams,
From the sewing machine,
Now I may look more like a patchwork doll-
But I'm trying to look at my past
As a tapestry made so that I can look back,
And feel proud
Of every time I chose to speak out.

Refuse to compromise:

Once I got my first taste
Of fresh, deep, clean oxygen
I knew that I had to make
Whatever sacrifice
To create a life
Where this air
Was always available.
If that meant talking it through,
If it meant letting go,
If it meant breaking,
If it meant healing,
Whatever it took-
I couldn't live
An oxygen depleted life
Anymore.

<u>Finally, rest.</u>

That shame
Used to rush
Through my veins.

Those words
Spoken in darkness
Left truth so blurred.

Those lies
Were sown into my soul
And reaped a wound I couldn't cauterize
On my own,

But then-
A spark of light
Illuminated the place
Where the shame
And his words,
And those lies,
Had lived.

At first
The magnitude of that damage
Had me running scared,
But slowly,
Slowly,
I began to make repairs.

Put a name
On that shame
And call it what it is.

Let my voice
And my choice
Be louder than the words he spoke.

Lay the truth
Like a balm to soothe
The aching and breaking those lies caused.

And then, dig three graves
For the lies, words, and shame
And with each secret voiced,
I make a conscious choice to confess
And to lay them each to a final rest.
I finally rest.

I finally rest.

Epilogue:

Even though this book is finished, it doesn't mean I am- this healing is a process, and I don't know how long the process will take, but I know the end result will be beautiful.

I want you to know, that even though you may feel shattered right now- your broken pieces can still create a stain glass window where the light can shine through. This dark won't last forever. This is just a season, and the thing about seasons is they change- if you hate the season you're in, hold on to the fact that it won't always be this way.

I don't know why it has to be so hard, but I do know that you're strong, you've made it this far, so chin up- because you and me? We're fighters, and we're gonna be okay.

"Those who plant in tears will harvest shouts of joy."
Psalm 126:5

Acknowledgments:

I would have never had the courage to write this book, to give these words to the world, and take up this space if it weren't for the huge support system that constantly reminds me that I am loved.

To those individuals who I call my friends, my tribe, my home, my safe haven- all summing up to one word, my family. Thank you for choosing me to be yours. Thank you for being mine.

Made in the USA
Lexington, KY
03 April 2019